THE STAN LEE

A Biography Book for New Readers

—— Written by ——
Frank Berrios

——— Illustrated by ———
Patrick Corrigan

ROCKRIDGE
PRESS

To Mom and Dad, who encouraged me to read everything. And to my grandmothers, who gave me Little Golden Books and comics to read on the subway.

Series Designer: Angela Navarra
Interior and Cover Designer: John Clifford
Art Producer: Tom Hood
Editor: Erum Khan
Production Editor: Jenna Dutton

Illustrations © Patrick Corrigan, 2021. Photographs Alamy, p. 48; Radharc Images/Alamy, p. 50; PictureLux/The Hollywood Archive/Alamy, p. 51

Author photograph courtesy of Mike Meskin

ISBN: Print 978-1-64876-092-1 | eBook 978-1-64876-093-8

R0

CONTENTS

CHAPTER 1

A CREATOR IS BORN

Meet Stan Lee

Stan Lee was a **comic book** creator with an incredible imagination. In the 1960s, along with amazing **artists** like Jack Kirby, Steve Ditko, and Don Heck, he created some of the most famous **superheroes** ever—the Fantastic Four, the Incredible Hulk, Spider-Man, Thor, Iron Man, Doctor Strange, the X-Men, Black Panther, and many more!

The characters that Stan helped create more than 60 years ago have made the stunning leap from the comic page into toys, books, video games, television shows, and movies! When he started in the comic book business at age 17, Stan never imagined any of those things would happen. He just liked working with talented artists and creating new characters with exciting stories.

As the **editor in chief** and then **publisher** of **Marvel Comics**, Stan became the public face

of the company and also a comic book **icon**. He
appeared in many Marvel Studios films and was
turned into an action figure. Stan even has a star
on the Hollywood Walk of Fame! So sit back,
true believer, and get ready to hear about the
amazing life of Stan Lee.

Stan's World

Stan was born in Manhattan, New York City,
on December 28, 1922. His parents named him
Stanley Martin Lieber. Life in New York was

difficult for most people during the 1920s. **Immigrants** from all over the world moved to the city with hopes of finding work. They often lived in small, crowded apartments with thin walls and little privacy. Despite the noise and overcrowding, these brand-new New Yorkers tried their best to make it their home.

But in October 1929, the **stock market** crashed. As a result, many

JUMP
—IN THE—
THINK TANK

Stan loved to draw and read all types of books as a child. What do you like to do when you have free time?

banks closed. Factories and stores went out of business. Millions of people across the country lost their jobs, including Stan's father. Like most Americans during the **Great Depression**, Stan's parents would have to figure out a way to get by with less and less. But Stan's parents encouraged Stan and his younger brother, Larry, to believe that better days were ahead.

Although life was sometimes hard, Stan found joy in books. He read just about anything he could get his hands on! He enjoyed comic strips like *Dick Tracy*, about a police detective with cool gadgets. He spent hours getting lost in **science fiction** stories by Jules Verne.

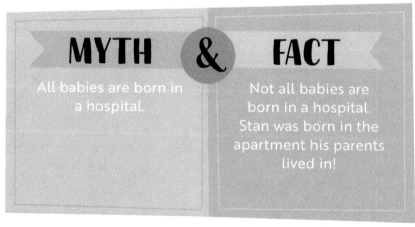

MYTH & FACT

All babies are born in a hospital.

Not all babies are born in a hospital. Stan was born in the apartment his parents lived in!

Mystery and adventure books about the Hardy Boys and Tarzan were also favorites. Stan even liked to read during meals! His mother bought him a little stand to keep his books open while he ate. Those stories would fuel his imagination and one day **inspire** him to create marvelous tales of his own.

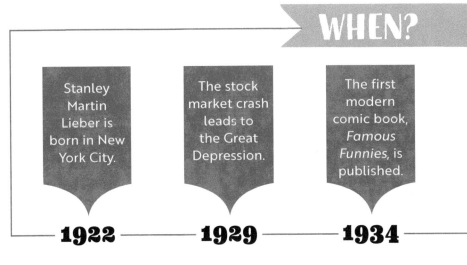

WHEN?

Stanley Martin Lieber is born in New York City.	The stock market crash leads to the Great Depression.	The first modern comic book, *Famous Funnies*, is published.
1922	**1929**	**1934**

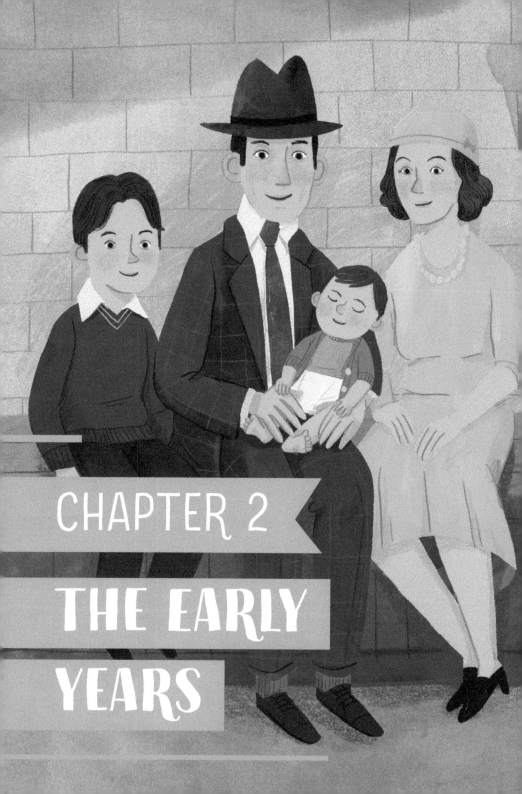

CHAPTER 2

THE EARLY YEARS

Growing Up

Stan's parents, Jack and Celia Lieber, were from Romania, a country in Europe. They had come to the United States with dreams of finding work, starting a family, and buying a home. But without a job, Stan's father struggled to pay the bills. The family had to live in a very small apartment. Stan never liked their home. The only window looked out at a brick wall. Stan dreamed of having an apartment with a window in the front of the building, where you could see everything that was going on outside.

Manhattan could be lonely in the summer without a car. Most of Stan's friends went to summer camp or the beach. With no money and no one around, the days felt long. But when Stan turned 12, he received a wonderful birthday present: a bicycle! He rode all over the neighborhood and let his imagination wander.

He would become a brave knight on a horse or the pilot of a spaceship!

Meanwhile, Stan's father tried everything to find a job, but nothing seemed to work.

My mother used to say that if there was nothing to read, I'd read the labels on ketchup bottles, which I did!

Stan saw how difficult life was for his father. It made him want to work hard for the rest of his life. Stan's mother urged him to finish school quickly so he could get a job and earn money to help the family.

The Lieber Family

ZANFIR SOLOMON (1861–1932)

SOPHIE HOFFMAN (1861–1925)

SIMON LIEBER (~1843–?)

MINNIE LEIBOWITZ (~1856–1891)

CELIA SOLOMON (1886–1947)

JACK LIEBER (1886–1968)

STANLEY MARTIN LIEBER (1922–2018)

LAWRENCE LIEBER (1931–)

JUMP
—IN THE—
THINK TANK

Do you like to dress up or pretend to be your favorite characters? If so, who do you pretend to be?

Stories and More Stories

When Stan was lucky enough to have a little money, he could be found at a local movie theater. *The Adventures of Robin Hood* was one of his favorite films. Stan loved to imagine himself as the hero of an exciting story.

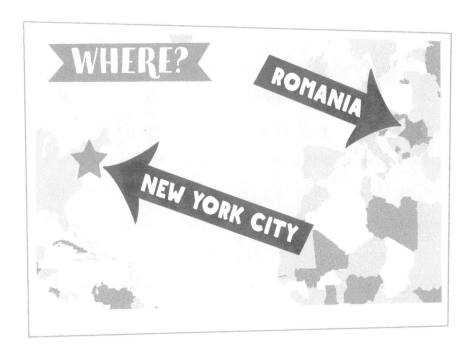

ROMANIA

NEW YORK CITY

Stan worked hard in school and even skipped a few grades. As the youngest kid in class, Stan didn't make many friends in high school. But he was inspired by one of his favorite teachers, Leon B. Ginsberg Jr. Mr. Ginsberg would use funny stories to keep his students interested in the lesson. Stan realized that learning could be fun and that humor was a great way to reach people.

To help his family, Stan found a few part-time jobs after school. He delivered sandwiches to offices and worked at a company that made pants. Stan hated that job, because no matter how hard he worked, no one took the time to learn his name.

When he was 15, Stan won prize money after entering a local newspaper's essay contest. The prize **motivated** Stan to become a **writer**!

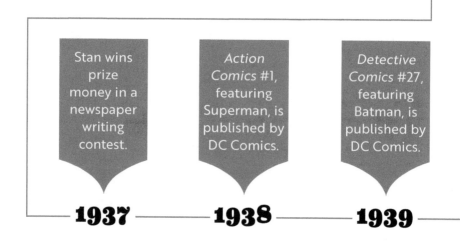

WHEN?

Stan wins prize money in a newspaper writing contest.	*Action Comics #1,* featuring Superman, is published by DC Comics.	*Detective Comics #27,* featuring Batman, is published by DC Comics.
1937	**1938**	**1939**

CHAPTER 3

STAN THE WRITER

The First Job

Stan graduated from high school at age 16. While other kids dreamed of college, Stan's family needed money right away. He began looking for a full-time job. Stan's uncle told him about a job at a **publishing company** called Timely Comics. It was owned by a man named Martin Goodman, who was married to Stan's cousin. A publishing company makes money by creating and selling books, comics, or **magazines**. Stan loved to read, so this felt like the perfect job for him.

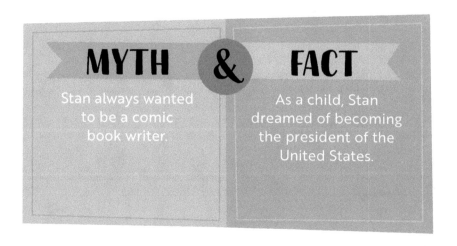

MYTH & FACT

Stan always wanted to be a comic book writer.

As a child, Stan dreamed of becoming the president of the United States.

Stan was hired by Joe Simon, the **editor** at Timely. Joe was a writer and artist, but as the editor, he was responsible for all the comic books Timely published. Joe worked closely with another writer and artist named Jack Kirby. For each comic, a writer would write the story first. Then an artist like Jack would figure out what the characters looked like by drawing sketches. Everything in the comic book would be drawn by the artist.

As the **gofer** at Timely, Stan had to get coffee and snacks for his busy coworkers. He would also do other small jobs, like reading the mail or **proofreading** pages to catch mistakes.

JUMP
—IN THE—
THINK TANK

What do you want to do after you graduate from high school? Do you want to go to college or get a job right away?

Becoming Stan Lee

After the success of Superman and Batman, created by **rival** publisher **DC Comics** a few years earlier, Martin Goodman published *Marvel Comics* #1. It featured two superheroes—a robotic man named the Human Torch, who could shoot fireballs from his hands, and Namor the Sub-Mariner, an angry prince of an underwater kingdom. Then Joe Simon and Jack Kirby created the hero known as Captain America. Captain America was an instant success, which gave Stan an opportunity. As Joe and Jack tried to keep up with the demand for new adventures for Captain America, Stan was asked to write a short story for a new issue.

Stan's first story was tucked into the back of the comic, but Stan didn't care. He was excited to write! But he also had dreams of writing **novels** like his childhood heroes, Charles Dickens and Mark Twain. So instead of using his real name,

Stan decided to use a **pen name** for his comic book stories. A pen name is a fake name that writers use instead of their real names. Stan decided to chop his first name, Stanley, in half and use Stan Lee as his pen name. That way, he could save his full name for the great things he planned to write one day.

Stan enjoyed working and learning under pros like Joe Simon and Jack Kirby. Before long, Joe and Jack grew unhappy with their jobs at Timely. When they suddenly left, Martin put 18-year-old Stan in charge as editor!

Stan graduates from high school.

1939

Stan gets a job at Timely Comics.

1939

Marvel Comics #1, featuring the Human Torch, is published.

1939

Captain America Comics #1 is published by Timely Comics.

1941

Stan's first story appears in *Captain America Comics* #3.

1941

Stan becomes editor at Timely.

1941

CHAPTER 4

BIG CHANGES

Off to War

As a young editor, it was hard for Stan to be taken seriously by writers and artists. But it was even harder for Stan to work on comic books while World War II was going on. It had begun when Germany took over Poland in 1939. When Japanese planes attacked American forces in Hawaii on December 7, 1941, the United States had no choice but to enter the war.

As other men his age went off to fight, it didn't feel right for Stan to stay home and work on comics. In 1942, he joined the United States Army. Because of his writing experience, Stan was asked to write **manuals** and **scripts** for Army training films. Stan's work for the Army kept him in the United States, far away from the fighting in Europe and Asia. Meanwhile, he still wrote stories for Timely. As other soldiers slept around him, Stan was busy writing comics at night.

Before long, Stan saved enough money to buy a **secondhand** car. When Stan was a kid, his family couldn't afford a car, so he was proud. When World War II came to an end in 1945, Stan quickly returned to New York so he could get back to work at Timely.

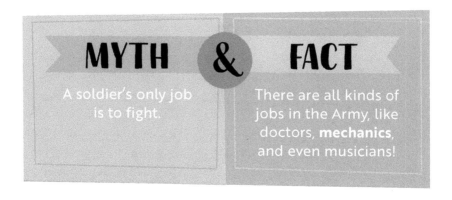

MYTH & FACT

A soldier's only job is to fight.

There are all kinds of jobs in the Army, like doctors, **mechanics**, and even musicians!

City Life

Stan was glad to be home in New York. He had a job he loved and was now making enough money to buy a brand-new car! Stan could hardly believe how much his life had changed in just a few years. With some cash in his pocket,

he was excited to explore the city. But instead
of taking a crowded bus or train, Stan enjoyed
walking. He would walk more than 40 blocks to
his office in the Empire State Building each day.

In 1947, Stan's life changed again when he met
Joan Clayton Boocock. Joan was from England,
but had moved to New York to work as a **model**.

JUMP
—IN THE—
THINK
TANK

What are your favorite places to go in your town or city?

For Stan, it was love at first sight! He called her by the nickname Joanie, and they were married before the end of the year.

Meanwhile, business was booming at Timely. Stan still wrote stories featuring superheroes like

Captain America and the Human Torch. He knew that most comic book readers were boys back then, but he also tried to get more girls to read comics by publishing stories with female superheroes like Namora and the Blonde Phantom. Stan tried teen humor and romance tales. Then he switched to mysteries and Western adventures. Stan enjoyed working on many different books, but instead of following the latest **trends**, he wanted to set new ones.

The United States enters World War II. **1941**

Stan joins the US Army. **1942**

World War II ends. **1945**

Stan returns to Timely Comics. **1945**

Stan marries Joan Clayton Boocock. **1947**

CHAPTER 5

THE WORLD OF COMICS

Tough Times

After their wedding, Stan and Joanie lived in a tiny Manhattan apartment. But when Stan's mother suddenly passed away, his 15-year-old brother, Larry, needed a place to live. Stan moved Joanie and Larry into a small house on Long Island. Soon after, Stan and Joanie's first daughter, Joan Celia Lee, was born. Stan was a proud father—he adored his baby girl. Three years later, Joan gave birth to a second daughter, Jan. Sadly, Jan passed away a few days after being born. Stan and Joanie were both very sad, but Joan Celia, or J. C. as she was later called, gave her parents the love, hope, and strength to carry on.

A few years earlier, Timely Comics had been renamed Atlas Comics. Stan still worked there, where he wrote story after story. He also worked on comics written by others. As a result, Stan

JUMP
—IN THE—
THINK
TANK

Where do you like to do your homework? In your room? At the kitchen table? Somewhere else?

had less and less time to write at the office. Stan asked his boss, Martin, if he could work from home several days a week, and Martin agreed. This allowed Stan to write even more stories and spend time with J. C. and Joanie.

Stan enjoyed working from home. During the summer, he would often

write in his backyard while standing up! But
he was unsure about his career. Most people
thought comic books were a silly waste of time.
Some even believed comics were bad for kids!
At parties, Stan was embarrassed to admit that
he wrote comic books. He often thought about
finding a new job.

The Comics Code

In 1954, a **psychiatrist** named Dr. Fredric
Wertham wrote a book that warned parents
to keep their children away from comics. He
thought comic books about **crime** had too much
violence and turned teenagers into **criminals**.
He also thought scary stories were bad for kids.
Stan disagreed. In the Army, he'd seen how
comic books had helped some soldiers learn

MYTH & FACT

MYTH: Comic books aren't educational.

FACT: You can learn all kinds of things from comic books! Most are **fiction**, but there are also **nonfiction** comic books about famous people and events in history.

how to read. Comic books also helped take their minds off the war, if only for a short time. But Dr. Wertham scared people. As more and more stores refused to sell comics, Stan had to cancel title after title. Then Martin told Stan to let go of the writers and artists who worked for them. Stan had to fire many people who had become his good friends. But Stan still felt lucky. While lots of companies were forced to go out of business, he still had a job.

To make parents feel better, comic book publishers created a group called the **Comics Code Authority**. The Comics Code Authority had to approve each and every comic book, judging it by a strict set of rules. If a comic followed the rules, it received the Comics Code Seal of Approval, which meant it was considered safe for kids to read. But if they thought a picture or story was violent, it had to be changed before most shops would agree to sell it.

WHEN?

| Stan and Joan's daughter, Joan Celia (J. C.), is born. | Timely Comics is renamed Atlas Comics. | Stan and Joan's second daughter, Jan, passes away. | The Comics Code Authority is created. |

1950 —— 1951 —— 1953 —— 1954 —

CHAPTER 6

THE MARVEL
YEARS

Superheroes Unite!

By 1960, Stan was ready to quit the comic business. But then rival publisher DC Comics scored a big hit with a comic book called *Justice League of America*. It featured a team of their most popular superheroes, including Batman, Superman, and Wonder Woman. Stan's boss, Martin, wanted him to create a similar comic book with a team of heroes featuring the Human Torch and Captain America. Stan was tired of copying others. Joanie suggested he write something fresh and new.

Stan followed his wife's advice, and for the first time in years, he was excited about comics again! He wanted to create new characters with interesting personalities. He also wanted them to have problems, like people in the real world. Stan wrote a story with his new characters, then asked his old friend Jack Kirby to bring them to life. Jack worked on the art, and in 1961, the

Fantastic Four became an instant success! Stan and Jack quickly followed up with a huge green-skinned hero called the Hulk in 1962.

Stan turned to another artist for his idea about a young hero who lived in Queens, New York. Steve Ditko was the perfect artist to draw the teenage crime-fighter known as Spider-Man. As the fan letters began to roll in, Stan and Martin decided it was time for a new company name. Martin had named Timely's first superhero comic book *Marvel Comics*. Stan liked the name, so on that day, Marvel Comics was born!

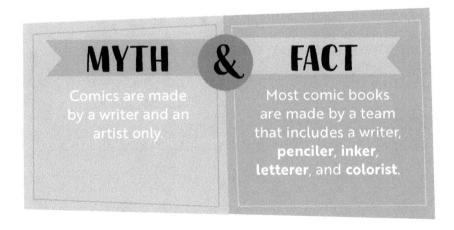

MYTH & FACT

Comics are made by a writer and an artist only.

Most comic books are made by a team that includes a writer, **penciler**, **inker**, **letterer**, and **colorist**.

The Marvel Method

Stan was on top of the world again. With a talented group of artists, Stan co-created new heroes like Thor, Iron Man, and the X-Men. Stan and Jack Kirby even created Black Panther, the first African superhero in comic books!

To keep up with the demand, Stan invented a new way to work. First, he would give the artist the basic **plot** of the story—a simple beginning, middle, and end. The artist was free to draw the story any way they wanted, as long as they followed Stan's plot. When they were done, Stan would add **dialogue** to the pages. This became known as the **Marvel Style**. Some publishers continue to work this way today! The Marvel Style gave artists freedom to be creative and kept them busy with steady work.

Stan also broke other rules. The Comics Code Authority told Stan he couldn't publish a Spider-Man story that told kids that drugs were bad. Stan published the comic books anyway, and they were an instant hit! Stan also came up with the idea of a continued **storyline** over several issues. Readers often waited a month to find out what happened to their favorite heroes and villains.

Stan was finally proud of the work he was
doing. When Martin decided to sell the company,
it was no surprise that Stan was asked to become
the new publisher of Marvel Comics.

Atlas Comics is renamed Marvel Comics.

1961

The Fantastic Four are created.

1961

The Incredible Hulk and Spider-Man are created.

1962

Iron Man is created.

1963

The X-Men are created.

1963

Black Panther is created.

1966

CHAPTER 7

STAN
THE LEGEND

Marvel in the Movies

As the publisher of Marvel Comics, Stan's new job was to make sure the company was successful. He traveled to colleges all over the country to meet fans. Stan hoped older readers would like his new stories, and he was right.

Marvel had already created several cartoons. But the success of DC's **live-action** *Batman* television show in the late 1960s gave Stan hope that Marvel could do the same with their characters. He was right again! In 1977, *The Incredible Hulk* television show was a hit with viewers of all ages.

Stan spent more and more time in Hollywood, where most movies and television shows were made. Soon, he began to think about moving there. Stan asked Marvel to send him to Los Angeles, where he could help their characters

JUMP
—IN THE—
THINK
TANK

Stan moved to Los Angeles after living in New York for most of his life. If you could move somewhere else, where would you go?

make the leap from the comic page to the movie screen. Stan loved the California sunshine, but found it difficult at first to get projects up and running. As a publisher, he had control over his ideas. In Hollywood, things were different. Some movies were written, but never made. Other films were badly made. Stan was frustrated.

WHERE?

IFORNIA

NEW YORK CITY

LOS ANGELES

Finally, in 1998, the first Marvel movie, *Blade*, was released. The movie made a lot of money. Suddenly everyone wanted to make a movie with Marvel! Two years later, the hugely successful *X-Men* film hit theaters. Stan even had a **cameo** in the film. Record-breaking films featuring Spider-Man, Iron Man, and many others would follow. Stan can be seen in almost every one of them!

Stan's Legacy

Though other people his age had stopped working years earlier, Stan could never really **retire**. He liked to stay busy. The comic legend attended many **comic book conventions**, where he would give talks, do **signings**, and take **selfies** with adoring fans. Stan appeared on TV shows like *The Simpsons* and *The Big Bang Theory*. He even hosted a **reality show** about superheroes!

Stan kept working until he died in 2018, but his **legacy** lives on. Comic books featuring superheroes and villains he co-created continue to be published. More than 20 Marvel Studios films have been made, including record-setting and

MYTH	&	FACT
You must retire when you get older.		Some people never retire! Stan loved to write, so he never wanted to retire.

award-winning films like *Iron Man, The Avengers,* and *Black Panther,* with more to come! People no longer think comics are silly or dangerous— teachers and librarians even use comics and **graphic novels** to help kids learn how to read!

As a comic book icon for more than 60 years, Stan inspired **generations** of writers, artists, and others with his amazing adventures. Stan Lee created heroes who could save the world. Today, many people see *him* as a true-life hero who changed their lives with his work.

WHEN?

The Incredible Hulk TV show premieres.

1977

Stan moves to Los Angeles.

about **1980**

Blade, the first Marvel movie, is released.

1998

The first *X-Men* movie is released.

2000

The first *Spider-Man* movie is released.

2002

Stan receives a star on Hollywood Walk of Fame.

2011

CHAPTER 8

SO...WHO WAS STAN LEE?

Challenge Accepted!

Now that you know so much about Stan Lee's life and work, let's test your knowledge with a little who, what, when, where, why, and how quiz. Feel free to look back in the text to find the answers if you need to, but try to remember first.

1. **Who was Stan Lee?**

   A A comic book colorist

   B A comic book letterer

   C A comic book penciler and inker

   D A comic book writer and editor

2. **What was Stan Lee's real name?**

   A Reed Richards

   B Peter Parker

   C Stanley Martin Lieber

   D Bruce Banner

3. **Where was Stan born?**

→ A Manhattan, New York

→ B Los Angeles, California

→ C Washington, DC

→ D Miami, Florida

4. **How old was Stan when he became the editor at Timely Comics?**

→ A 15

→ B 18

→ C 21

→ D 25

5. **Some people thought comic books were bad for kids. What is the name of the group that had to make sure comics were okay for kids to read?**

→ A The Avengers

→ B The Justice League

→ C The Comics Code Authority

→ D The X-Men

6. **WhatdidStanjoinduring World War II?**

→ A Army
→ B Navy
→ C Air Force
→ D Marines

7. **Which character did Stan NOT co-create?**

→ A Spider-Man
→ B Iron Man
→ C Batman
→ D Black Panther

8. **Which artists did Stan work with to create the Hulk, Spider-Man, and Iron Man?**

→ A Jack Kirby
→ B Steve Ditko
→ C Don Heck
→ D All of the above

9. What is the name of the comic book company Stan made famous around the world?

→ A DC Comics

→ B Marvel Comics

→ C Archie Comics

→ D Milestone Comics

10. How did Stan change the world?

→ A By writing amazing stories and co-creating incredible characters

→ B By inspiring people with his hard work

→ C By entertaining people with his movie appearances

→ D All of the above

Our World

Stan Lee was one of the biggest comic legends of all time. Let's look at some of the ways he helped to shape our world today.

→ Stan dreamed of doing big things as a child. He thought about being a writer, an actor, or even the president of the United States! Instead, he co-created the **Marvel Universe**—a place filled with awesome heroes and stunning villains that would entertain generations of fans to come.

→ Stan changed the game! People thought comics were just for kids. Then Stan showed the world that amazing stories for readers of all ages could be told using pictures and words together.

→ Stan stood up against **hatred** and **bigotry**. Stan Lee and Jack Kirby created Black Panther in 1966, during the **civil rights movement**. They wanted to show the country that anyone could be a hero, regardless of their race.

→ Stan made comics cool! Today, comic books are used in schools and studied in colleges. They've been turned into blockbuster movies that excite and amaze fans around the world.

JUMP
—IN THE—
THINK
TANK
FOR

MORE!

Now let's think a little more about what Stan did
and how he impacted the world we live in today.

→ Stan loved to tell stories with a lesson. In the very
first Spider-Man story, the young hero learns that "with
great power comes great **responsibility**." You have great
power, too! What can you do to change your world and
make it better? Can you help a neighbor or do something
nice for a brother, sister, or friend?

→ How can you embrace **diversity**? At times, we all feel
alone, or different. Remember, the things that make us
different also make us stronger, just like the Fantastic
Four! Don't be afraid to make a new friend and learn
more about the world.

→ What can you do to inspire others? Do you work hard
and tell the truth? Are you fair and like to share? If so,
that makes you a hero already. Keep up the good work!

Glossary

artist: A person who can sing, dance, act, write, paint, or draw

bigotry: Unwillingness to accept that every human being deserves the same basic rights

cameo: A very brief appearance in a film or television show

civil rights movement: A time of struggle during the 1950s and 1960s when Black people in the United States fought to end racial discrimination and have equal rights

colorist: An artist who adds color to a comic book

comic book: A booklet of stories told using words and pictures together

Comics Code Authority: A group formed when parents worried that comics were bad for kids to read

comic book conventions: Public gatherings of comic and movie fans

crime: An act that is against the law

criminal: A person who breaks the law

DC Comics: The publishing company that produces Superman, Batman, and Wonder Woman comic books

dialogue: The words spoken by characters on a comic book page

diversity: Inclusion and equal treatment for people of all races and cultures

editor: The person who hires the writers and artists and makes sure a story is done well

editor in chief: The person who hires the editors of a publishing company and makes sure the company earns money

fiction: A story that is made up or invented by a writer, using their imagination

generation: A group of people born and living around the same time

gofer: A person who "goes for" coffee and snacks and does other small jobs for their coworkers

graphic novel: A longer comic book story or collection of comic books

Great Depression: A worldwide financial crisis that started in 1929 and lasted nearly 10 years

hatred: Extreme dislike and bad treatment of others

icon: A person who is known and admired by many people

immigrant: A person born in one country who moves to another country and settles there

inker: An artist who adds detail to the penciled artwork so it can be copied by the printer

inspire: To influence, move, or guide someone by words or example

legacy: A gift from someone who has died; can be physical or nonphysical, like an idea, information, or a system

letterer: An artist who adds the words, balloons, and sound effects to a comic book page

live-action: Movies or television shows created with actors, instead of animation or cartoons

magazine: A monthly publication of news and other stories, similar to a newspaper

manual: A book that explains how to do something in a simple way

Marvel Bullpen: The nickname for the artists who create Marvel comic books

Marvel Comics: The publishing company that Stan Lee worked for, which produces the Fantastic Four, Avengers, X-Men, and Spider-Man comic books

Marvel Style: A way of working on comic books created by Stan Lee. To keep many artists working at the same time, Stan gave them the basic plot of each story. Artists had the freedom to add interesting characters and details. Then, when the art was finished, Stan would add dialogue and sound effects.

Marvel Universe: The fictional universe created by Stan Lee, Jack Kirby, Steve Ditko, and countless others, where heroes like the Avengers and the X-Men fight for good

mechanic: A person who repairs machines and motors, like cars or trucks

model: A person who poses for pictures to sell things like clothes or shoes

motivate: To give a person a reason to act

nonfiction: A story about things that have really happened

novel: A book-length fictional story

penciler: An artist who draws the characters on a comic book page, in pencil, based on the script from a writer

pen name: The fake name a writer uses when they don't want to use their real name

plot: The basic arc of a story, with a beginning, middle, and end

proofread: To read and check for mistakes

psychiatrist: A doctor who works with people who need mental or emotional support

publisher: A person who creates and sells comics, magazines, or books

publishing company: A business that creates and sells comics, magazines, or books

reality show: A television show featuring regular people instead of actors

responsibility: Something or someone that a person is in charge of and has to take care of

retire: To stop working, usually when a person turns 65 years old or older

rival: A person or company trying to compete for the same thing

science fiction: Made-up stories about real or imaginary science

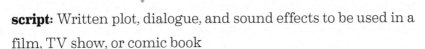

script: Written plot, dialogue, and sound effects to be used in a film, TV show, or comic book

secondhand: Owned by someone else before you

selfie: A photograph someone takes of themselves, sometimes with others

signing: A public gathering where fans can meet writers and artists to get their autograph or a selfie

stock market: A place where people and companies invest in and trade on other businesses

storyline: The plot, or beginning, middle, and end of a story

superhero: A fictional character with amazing powers or abilities

trend: A popular interest

violence: The use of physical force to harm someone

writer: A person who creates characters and stories

Bibliography

Batchelor, Bob. *Stan Lee: The Man Behind Marvel.* Lanham, MD: Rowman & Littlefield, 2017.

Howe, Sean. *Marvel Comics: The Untold Story.* New York: Harper Perennial, 2013.

Lee, Stan. *Stan Lee's How to Write Comics.* New York: Watson-Guptill Publications, 2011.

Lee, Stan, and Peter David. *Amazing Fantastic Incredible: A Marvelous Memoir.* New York: Gallery Books, 2015.

Lee, Stan, and George Mair. *Excelsior! The Amazing Life of Stan Lee.* New York: Fireside, 2002.

Maslon, Laurence, and Michael Kantor. *Superheroes!: Capes, Cowls, and the Creation of Comic Book Culture.* New York: Crown Archetype, 2013.

Wiacek, Stephen. *Black Panther: The Ultimate Guide.* New York: DK, 2018.

Acknowledgments

Comic books are mostly a collaborative effort, so you absolutely must mention artists like Jack Kirby and Steve Ditko when you talk about Stan Lee. But there are also many people in the Marvel Bullpen who worked silently on the comics, so I'd like to acknowledge all the nameless pencilers, inkers, letterers, and colorists (as well as the editorial staff!) who helped make Marvel what it is today.

I'd also like to thank my family—my parents and grandparents, for always encouraging me to read. To my sister and brother, for putting up with my ever-expanding comic collection over the years. To my Titis, cousins, nephews, and nieces, who inspire me each and every day to keep writing. And last, but not least, to Monk, who makes sure I always get the job done. **—FB**

About the Author

FRANK BERRIOS is a writer and editor. He was born and raised in New York City, just like Stan Lee! His love of comic books started early—in fact, Spider-Man was one of his favorite superheroes. Frank went on to become an assistant editor at DC Comics, where he worked with many people who had learned the comic business from Stan Lee himself. He has written many books for children, including the following Little Golden Books: *Black Panther*, *The Amazing Spider-Man*, *Falcon*, *Miles Morales: Spider-Man*, as well as *A Little Golden Book about Jackie Robinson*, *Football with Dad*, and *Soccer with Mom*. He enjoys biking, sketching, and collecting classic toys and comics. Learn more about his work at FrankBerriosBooks.com.

About the Illustrator

PATRICK CORRIGAN was born on a crisp, cold December day in a small, cloudy town in Cheshire, England. With a passion for precision as a child, he grew up patiently drawing and designing arts and crafts.

This took him to study ceramics at university, train as an art teacher, and eventually become an art director at a busy design studio where he would work for nearly 10 years. While there, he honed his skills working on more than 500 educational and picture books for children as well as animations and branding.

Now based in Hammersmith, West London—where he lives with his newspaper editor wife, Dulcie, and their fat cat, Forbes—Patrick uses Photoshop, Illustrator, and sometimes even real art equipment to create his work. He draws best when listening to his vast collection of vinyl that he often hides from his wife.

WHO WILL INSPIRE YOU NEXT?

EXPLORE A WORLD OF HEROES AND ROLE MODELS IN
THE STORY OF... BIOGRAPHY SERIES FOR NEW READERS.

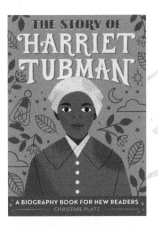

LOOK FOR THIS SERIES
WHEREVER BOOKS AND EBOOKS ARE SOLD

Alexander Hamilton	Jane Goodall
Albert Einstein	Barack Obama
Martin Luther King Jr.	Simone Biles
Jim Henson	Marie Curie

CPSIA information can be obtained
at www.ICGtesting.com
Printed in the USA
JSHW041520090122
21854JS00005B/9